COUNTRY

Formal Name: Republic of Cuba (República de Cuba).

Short Form: Cuba.

Term for Citizen(s): Cuban(s).

Click to Enlarge Image

Capital: La Habana (Havana). Term for residents: Habaneros (males), Habaneras (females).

Major Cities: Cuba's six largest cities (more than 200,000 inhabitants) in order of population (2005 estimates, not including urban agglomerations) are Havana (2,201,610), Santiago de Cuba (423,392), Camagüey (301,574), Holguín (269,618), Santa Clara (210,220), and Guantánamo (208,145).

Independence: Cuba attained its independence on May 20, 1902. It became independent from Spain on December 10, 1898, but was administered by the United States from 1898 to 1902.

Public Holidays: Fixed official holidays are Liberation Day (January 1); Victory of the Armed Forces (January 2); International Workers' Day (May 1); Eve of Revolution Day (July 25); Anniversary of the Moncada Barracks Attack Day, Revolution Day (July 26); Revolution Day, 2nd Day (July 27); Commencement of Wars of Independence Day (October 10); Independence Day (December 10); and Christmas Day (December 25).

Flag: The Cuban flag has five equal horizontal bands of blue (top, center, and bottom) alternating with white; a red equilateral triangle based on the hoist side bears a white, five-pointed star in the center.

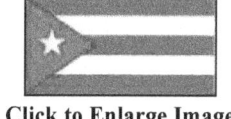

Click to Enlarge Image

HISTORICAL BACKGROUND

Colonial Rule: The history of Cuba began with the arrival of Christopher Columbus in 1492 and the subsequent invasion of the island by the Spaniards. Aboriginal groups—the Guanahatabey, Ciboney, and Taíno—inhabited the island but were soon eliminated or died as a result of diseases or the shock of conquest. Thus, the impact of indigenous groups on subsequent Cuban society was limited, and Spanish culture, institutions, language, and religion prevailed. Colonial society developed slowly after Spain colonized the island in the sixteenth and seventeenth centuries; pastoral pursuits and agriculture served as the basis of the economy. For the first three centuries after the conquest, the island remained a neglected stopping point for the Spanish fleet, which visited the New World and returned to Spain with the mineral wealth of continental America.

Cuba awakened dramatically in the nineteenth century. The growth of the United States as an independent nation, the collapse of Haiti as a sugar-producing colony, Spanish protective policies, and the ingenuity of Cuba's Creole business class all converged to produce a sugar revolution on the island. In a scant few years, Cuba was transformed from a sleepy, unimportant island into the major sugar producer in the world. Slaves arrived in increasing numbers; large estates squeezed out smaller ones; sugar supplanted tobacco, agriculture, and cattle as the main occupation; prosperity replaced poverty; and Spain's attention replaced neglect. These factors, especially the latter two, delayed a move toward independence in the early nineteenth century. While most of Latin America was breaking with Spain, Cuba remained loyal.

The Independence Struggle and Beginning of U.S. Hegemony: Toward the end of the nineteenth century, Cuban loyalty began to change as a result of Creole rivalry with Spaniards for the governing of the island, increased Spanish despotism and taxation, and the growth of Cuban nationalism. These developments combined to produce a prolonged and bloody war, the Ten Years' War against Spain (1868–78), but it failed to win independence for Cuba. At the outset of the second independence war (1895–98), Cuban independence leader José Martí was killed. As a result of increasingly strained relations between Spain and the United States, the Americans entered the conflict in 1898. Already concerned about its economic interests on the island and its strategic interest in a future Panama Canal, the United States was aroused by an alarmist "yellow" press after the USS *Maine* sank in Havana Harbor on February 15 as the result of an explosion of undetermined origin. In December 1898, with the Treaty of Paris, the United States emerged as the victorious power in the Spanish-American War, thereby ensuring the expulsion of Spain and U.S. tutelage over Cuban affairs.

On May 20, 1902, after almost five years of U.S. military occupation, Cuba launched into nationhood with fewer problems than most Latin American nations. Prosperity increased during the early years. Militarism seemed curtailed. Social tensions were not profound. Yet corruption, violence, and political irresponsibility grew. Invoking the 1901 Platt Amendment, which was named after Senator Orville H. Platt and stipulated the right of the United States to intervene in Cuba's internal affairs and to lease an area for a naval base in Cuba, the United States intervened militarily in Cuba in 1906–9, 1917, and 1921. U.S. economic involvement also weakened the growth of Cuba as a nation and made the island more dependent on its northern neighbor.

Rising Authoritarianism, 1901–1930s: The 1930s saw a major attempt at revolution. Prompted by the cruel dictatorship of Gerardo Machado y Morales (president, 1925–33), the economic hardships of the world depression, and the growing control of their economy by Spaniards and North Americans, a group of Cubans led by students and intellectuals sought radical reforms and a profound transformation of Cuban society. Following several small army revolts, Machado was forced to resign and flee the country on August 12, 1933. Sergeant Fulgencio Batista y Zaldívar, unhappy with proposed reductions of pay and restrictions of promotions, joined forces with the militant students on September 4 and overthrew the U.S.-backed regime of Carlos Manuel de Céspedes (the younger). By making the military part of the government and allowing Batista to emerge as self-appointed chief of the armed forces, the Sergeants' Revolt marked a turning point in Cuba's history. On January 14, 1934, Army Chief Batista also brought to an end the short-lived provisional presidency of Ramón Grau San Martín (president, 1933–34) by forcing him to resign. Although the reformers attained power five months later and Machado's overthrow was supposed to mark the beginning of an era of reform, their revolution failed. Batista (president, 1940–44; dictator, 1952–59) and the military emerged as the arbiters of Cuba's politics, first through de facto ruling and finally with the election of Batista to the presidency in 1940.

The end of the early Batista era during World War II was followed by an era of democratic government, respect for human rights, and accelerated prosperity under the inheritors of the 1933 revolution—Grau San Martín (president, 1944–48) and Carlos Prío Socarrás (president, 1948–52). Yet political violence and corruption increased. Many saw these administrations of the Cuban Revolutionary Party (Partido Revolucionario Cubano—PRC), more commonly known as the Authentic Party (Partido Auténtico), as having failed to live up to the ideals of the revolution. Others still supported the Auténticos and hoped for new leadership that could correct the vices of the past. A few conspired to take power by force.

The Rise of Fidel Castro: Batista's coup d'état on March 10, 1952, had a profound effect on Cuban society, leading to doubts about the ability of the Cubans to govern themselves. It also began a brutal right-wing dictatorship that resulted in the polarization of society, civil war, the overthrow of Batista, and the destruction of the military and most other Cuban institutions. Fidel Castro Ruz, a charismatic, anti-U.S. revolutionary, seized power on January 1, 1959, following his successful revolt against the U.S.-backed Batista government. As the Castro regime expropriated U.S. properties and investments and began, officially, on April 16, 1961, to convert Cuba into a one-party communist system, relations between the United States and Cuba deteriorated rapidly. The United States imposed an embargo on Cuba on October 19,1960, and broke diplomatic relations on January 3, 1961, in response to Castro's expropriations without compensation and other provocations, such as arrests of U.S. citizens. The failure of the Central Intelligence Agency (CIA)–sponsored invasion by Cuban exiles in April 1961 (the infamous Bay of Pigs invasion) allowed the Castro regime to destroy the entire Cuban underground and to emerge strengthened and consolidated, basking in the huge propaganda value of having defeated the "Yankees."

The Cold War Period: Tensions between the two governments peaked during the Cuban Missile Crisis of October 1962 after the United States revealed the presence of Soviet missiles in Cuba. Following the imposition of a U.S. naval blockade, the weapons were withdrawn and the missile bases dismantled, thus resolving one of the most serious international crises since World War II. A U.S.-Soviet agreement that ended the Cuban Missile Crisis assured Cuba's protection from military attack by the United States.

Cuba's alliance with the Soviets provided a protective umbrella that propelled Castro onto the international scene. Cuba's support of anti-U.S. guerrilla and terrorist groups in Latin America and other countries of the developing world, military intervention in Africa, and unrestricted Soviet weapons deliveries to Cuba suddenly made Castro an important international contender. Cuba's role in bringing to power a Marxist regime in Angola in 1975 and in supporting the Sandinista overthrow of the dictatorship of Nicaragua's Anastasio Somoza Debayle in July 1979 perhaps stand out as Castro's most significant accomplishments in foreign policy. In the 1980s, the U.S. military expulsion of the Cubans from Grenada, the electoral defeat of the Sandinistas in Nicaragua, and the peace accords in El Salvador and Central America showed the limits of

Cuba's influence and "internationalism" (Cuban missions to support governments or insurgencies in the developing world).

A Continuing Cuban-U.S. Cold War: The collapse of communism in the early 1990s had a profound effect on Cuba. Soviet economic subsidies to Cuba ended as of January 1, 1991. Without Soviet support, Cuba was submerged in a major economic crisis. The gross national product contracted by as much as one-half between 1989 and 1993, exports fell by 79 percent and imports by 75 percent, the budget deficit tripled, and the standard of living of the population declined sharply. The Cuban government refers to the economic crisis of the 1990s and the austerity measures put in place to try to overcome it euphemistically as the "special period in peacetime." Minor adjustments, such as more liberalized foreign investment laws and the opening of private (but highly regulated) small businesses and agricultural stands, were introduced. Yet the regime continued to cling to an outdated Marxist and *caudillista* (dictatorial) system, refusing to open the political process or the economy.

The traditional Cold War hostility between Cuba and the United States continued unabated during the 1990s, and illegal Cuban immigration to the United States and human rights violations in Cuba remained sensitive issues. As the post-Soviet Cuban economy imploded for lack of once-generous Soviet subsidies, illegal emigration became a growing problem. The 1994 *balsero* crisis (named after the makeshift rafts or other unseaworthy vessels used by thousands of Cubans) constituted the most significant wave of Cuban illegal emigrants since the Mariel Boatlift of 1980, when 125,000 left the island. A Cuban-U.S. agreement to limit illegal emigration had the unintended effect of making alien smuggling of Cubans into the United States a major business.

In 1996 the U.S. Congress passed the so-called Helms–Burton law, introducing tougher rules for U.S. dealings with Cuba and deepening economic sanctions. The most controversial part of this law, which led to international condemnation of U.S. policy toward Cuba, involved sanctions against third-party nations, corporations, or individuals that trade with Cuba. The U.S. stance toward Cuba became progressively more hard-line, as demonstrated by the appointment of several prominent Cuban-Americans to the administration of George W. Bush. Nevertheless, as a result of pressure from European countries, particularly Spain, the Bush administration continued the Clinton administration's policy of suspending a provision in the Helms–Burton Act that would allow U.S. citizens and companies to sue foreign firms using property confiscated from them in Cuba during the 1959 Revolution. Instead, the Bush administration sought to increase pressure on the Castro regime through increased support for domestic dissidents and new efforts to broadcast pro-U.S. messages to Cubans and to bypass Cuba's jamming of U.S. television and radio broadcasts to Cuba.

Several incidents in 2000–1 involving Cuban spies also underscored the continuing Cuban-U.S. cold war. In addition, in early 2002 the Bush administration began to make a concerted effort to isolate Cuba from traditionally sympathetic Latin American countries such as Mexico, but Cuba has continued to have diplomatic and trade relations with Latin America. Although the successful visit to Havana in May 2002 by former U.S. president Jimmy Carter brought renewed efforts in Congress to lift the embargo, President Bush reaffirmed his support for it and sought to more strictly enforce the U.S. ban on travel by Americans to Cuba. In January 2004, he canceled immigration talks with Havana that had been held biannually for a decade. In May 2004, he endorsed new proposals to reduce the amount of remittances émigrés can send back to Cuba and further restrict the number of visits Cubans living in the United States can make to their homeland. Cuba responded by cultivating closer relations with China and North Korea.

Internal Political Developments: A crack opened in the Cuban system in May 2002, when a petition with 11,000 signatures—part of an unusual dissident initiative known as the Varela Project—was submitted to the National Assembly of Popular Power (hereafter, National Assembly). Started by Oswaldo José Payá Sadinas, now Cuba's most prominent dissident leader, the Varela Project called for a referendum on basic civil and political liberties and a new electoral law. In the following month, however, the government responded by initiating a drive to mobilize popular support for an amendment to the constitution, subsequently adopted unanimously by the National Assembly, declaring the socialist system to be "untouchable," permanent, and "irrevocable."

In recent years, Cuban politics have been dominated by a government campaign targeting negative characteristics of the socialist system, such as "indiscipline" (for example, theft of public and private property, absenteeism, and delinquency), corruption, and negligence. Under the campaign, unspecified indiscipline-related charges were brought against a member of the Cuban Communist Party and its Political Bureau, resulting in his dismissal from these positions in April 2006.

One of the world's last unyielding communist bulwarks, Castro, hospitalized by an illness, transferred power provisionally to his brother, General Raúl Castro Ruz, first vice president of the Council of State and Council of Ministers and minister of the Revolutionary Armed Forces on July 31, 2006. Fidel Castro's unprecedented transfer of power and his prolonged recovery appeared to augur the end of the Castro era.

GEOGRAPHY

Click to Enlarge Image

Location: Cuba is located between the Caribbean Sea and the North Atlantic Ocean. It is the westernmost island of the Greater Antilles and the largest country in the Caribbean. Its nearest Caribbean neighbors, listed clockwise, are The Bahamas, Haiti (separated from Cuba by the Windward Passage), Jamaica, and the Cayman Islands. Cuba is separated from the southern tip of Florida by the Strait of Florida and from the easternmost tip of Mexico by the Yucatan Channel.

Size: Cuba is slightly smaller than Pennsylvania. Its land area is 110,860 square kilometers, including Isla de Cuba (104,945 square kilometers), Isla de la Juventud (2,200 square kilometers), and adjacent keys (3,715 square kilometers). The island extends about 1,225 kilometers from Cabo de San Antonio to Cabo Mais, the western and eastern extremities, respectively. The average width is about 80 kilometers, with extremes ranging from 35 to 251 kilometers.

Land Boundaries: Cuba has a total land boundary of 29 kilometers bordering the U.S. naval base at Guantánamo Bay.

Disputed Territory: The United States has leased the Guantánamo Bay naval base area from Cuba since 1903, but the Castro regime has never recognized the legitimacy of the leasing arrangement. Although the 1901 Platt Amendment was repealed in 1934, the 1903 lease agreement has continued as a result of the Treaty of Relations signed by the United States and Cuba in 1934.

Length of Coastline: Cuba, with more than 4,000 coves and inlets, has an irregular coastline that is 3,209 kilometers on its northern side and 2,537 kilometers on its southern side, for a total of 5,746 kilometers. The coastline of Isla de La Juventud is 327 kilometers long.

Maritime Claims: As a signatory to the Law of the Sea Treaty, Cuba claims a 12-nautical-mile territorial sea and a 200-nautical-mile exclusive economic zone.

Topography: Cuba is a long but relatively narrow island. About two-thirds of its land surface is covered with fertile plains suitable for cultivation; three principal, heavily forested mountain ranges cover the rest of the country. The Sierra de los Órganos, which rises to a maximum elevation of about 686 meters, lies to the west of Havana. Toward the center of the island is the Sierra de Trinidad, which reaches a maximum elevation of 1,006 meters and together with the Sierra de Sancti Spíritus constitutes the Sierra de Escambray. Still farther east lies the island's highest and most rugged mountain range, the Sierra Maestra, which encircles the city of Santiago de Cuba and includes Cuba's highest peak, the Pico Real del Turquino (1,974 meters). Large tracts of mangrove swamp are particularly prevalent in the south and southwest, whereas the northern coastline is steep and rocky.

Principal Rivers: Cuba has 30 south-flowing and 11 north-flowing rivers with a total length of 3,932 kilometers. The average length of Cuba's major rivers, none of which are navigable to any significant extent, is 93 kilometers. The island's longest river is the 370-kilometer Cauto, which flows from the eastern mountains to the southern coast and is navigable for about 80 kilometers. Cuba's most important hydrographic basins are the Cauto, Zaza, and Sagua la Grande.

Climate: Cuba's climate is subtropical, warm, and humid; annual mean temperatures average 25° C. The hottest month in Havana (24 meters above sea level) is August, with an average monthly minimum of 24° C to 32° C; the coldest months are January and February, averaging 18° C to 27° C (with occasional freezing temperatures in mountainous areas). Cuba's average annual rainfall is 1,400 millimeters, but the annual amount varies greatly from year to year. The driest months are February and March, averaging 46 millimeters of rainfall. The wettest month is October, with average rainfall of 173 millimeters. Most of Cuba experiences a rainy season from May to October. The country averages about one hurricane every other year. The most frequent storms occur in September and October, but hurricane season generally runs from June to November (from August to November on the east coast). Heavy rains may cause landslides in hills and mountain slopes in the highlands.

Natural Resources: In addition to arable land, Cuba's natural resources include chromium, cobalt, copper, iron ore, manganese, natural gas, nickel (the world's second largest reserves), petroleum, salt silica, and timber. Although generally considered to be poorly endowed with energy resources, Cuba is one of only three countries in the Caribbean with significant oil and gas reserves; proven hydrocarbon reserves in 2005 totaled 750 million barrels of oil and 2.5 billion cubic feet of natural gas. In 2005 Cuba announced its first new discovery of oil since 1999—a reserve of 100 million barrels located 54 kilometers from Havana. The U.S. Geological Survey has estimated that Cuban territorial waters in the Gulf of Mexico could contain at least 4.6 billion barrels of oil and 9.8 trillion cubic feet of natural gas.

Land Use: Two-thirds of Cuba, or about 6,686,700 hectares, is covered with fertile plains suitable for cultivation; at least 3,701,400 hectares, and as much as 60 percent of the total arable land, are cultivated for agriculture. About 12 percent of agricultural land contains highly productive, deep, and permeable soils; about a fifth of the land is marginal for agriculture and is kept as meadows and pastures. The state controls about one-quarter of agricultural land and the nonstate sector, about three-quarters. Of the country's remaining uncultivated land, about a fifth is pasture or fallow and about a quarter forested. Human settlements account for 6.3 percent (or 694,000 hectares).

Environmental Factors: Water contamination with raw sewage, industrial waste, and agricultural run-off is the country's most significant environmental problem. Cuba has avoided some ecological calamities, such as beach erosion, while managing to partially reverse others, such as deforestation. Nevertheless, deforestation is becoming an increasingly important environmental issue in Cuba. In addition to combating this problem and biodiversity loss through reforestation and preservation programs, another important component of the government's strategy is prevention of forest fires, a leading cause of the forest destruction in Cuba. Frequent drought-like conditions have affected agriculture and resulted in more forest fires. Overhunting is also threatening the wildlife populations. The sugar industry has been the biggest source of industrial pollution, followed by the nickel refining industry. Cement factories in several cities including Havana are also a source of air pollution. Cuba's water supplies have been generally abundant, but water reserves were exceptionally low at the end of 2005 following several years of low rainfall, particularly in the eastern provinces.

Time Zone: Cuba is in the Standard Time zone, five hours behind Greenwich Mean Time (GMT–5) or four hours behind GMT from the last Sunday of March to the last Sunday of October, when daylight saving time is in effect.

SOCIETY

Population: According to Cuba's third post-1959 Population and Housing Census conducted in 2002, the island's permanent residents numbered 11,177,743, an increase of 1,454,138 inhabitants since the previous census in 1981. Cuba's estimated population in mid-2005 was 11,346,670. During 1990–2003, Cuba's annual population growth averaged less than 0.5 percent per year, well below the Latin American average of 1.6 percent. However, the population growth rate in 2002 and 2003 was 2.8 percent and 2.6 percent, respectively. According to the 2002 census, 75.9 percent of the total population was living in urban areas in cities ranging from 20,000 inhabitants to 100,000 or more. The provinces with at least 1 million estimated inhabitants in 2004 were Ciudad de La Habana (City of Havana), with 2.8 million; Holguín, 1 million; and Santiago de Cuba, 1 million. The country's official population density in 2003 was 101.3 inhabitants per square kilometer, but that figure had risen to an estimated 102.4 inhabitants per square kilometer by 2006, ranking Cuba number 72 of 238 in a list of countries with the densest populations.

Demography: Demographic indicators in 2006 included the following: a total fertility rate of an estimated 1.66 children born per woman, an estimated birthrate of 11.9 births per 1,000 population, a general mortality rate of 6.22 per 1,000 population, a death rate of an estimated 7.2 deaths per 1,000 population, and an infant mortality rate of 6.2 deaths per 1,000 live births. Deaths among children under five years of age (1.7 percent of all deaths) totaled 8.0 per 1,000 live births in 2003. Life expectancy at birth in 2006 was an estimated 77.4 years: 75.1 years for men and 79.8 years for women. After two decades of sustained declines in fertility and mortality rates, in 2003 the country was showing a process of aging: 14.7 percent of inhabitants were aged 60 or older, and persons under 15 years of age constituted only about 22 percent of the population. The average age of the population was 35.1. According to the 2002 census, the population is about equally divided between males and females.

Ethnic Groups and Languages: A multiracial society, Cuba has a population of mainly Spanish and African origins; a majority of inhabitants, 51 percent, are mulatto or mestizo; 37 percent, white; and 11 percent, black. A small Chinese minority constitutes less than 1 percent of the total population. Cuba has two living languages. Spanish (Español) is the official and dominant language. Lucumí is an ethnic language with Niger–Congo, Atlantic–Congo, Volta–Congo, Benue–Congo, Defoid, Yoruboid, and Edekiri roots.

Religion: Cuba has no official religion and is officially a secular state. In 1991 the Communist Party of Cuba (Partido Comunista de Cuba—PCC) lifted its prohibition against religious believers seeking membership, and a year later the constitution was amended to characterize the state as secular rather than atheist. Nevertheless, the government, through the Ministry of Interior's Office of Religious Affairs, restricts religious freedom. Although state restrictions apply to the independent Roman Catholic Church, they are enforced mainly against unregistered religious groups.

About 85 percent of the population was nominally Roman Catholic before Fidel Castro seized power. Although Roman Catholicism continues to be the largest organized religion, after more than four decades of an atheist regime, most young people are not religious, nor do they have any religious training. At the time of the Revolution, there were also small Protestant minorities, and Evangelical Protestant denominations have continued to grow rapidly. A small and dwindling Jewish community remains as well. Afro-Christian rites are widely practiced by Cubans of all races, but primarily blacks and mulattoes. The Lucumí rite, or Santería, is a religion originating in West African Yoruba culture. It remains widespread in Cuba regardless of people's nominal religious affiliation and state efforts to suppress it.

Education and Literacy: Public education in Cuba is universal and free through the university level. It is based on Marxist-Leninist principles and combines study with manual labor. Day nurseries are available for all children after their forty-fifth day, and national schools at the preprimary level are operated by the state for children of five years of age. Primary education from six to 11 years of age—or until the ninth grade—is compulsory, and secondary education lasts from 12 to 17 years of age, comprising two cycles of three years each. All elementary and secondary school students receive obligatory ideological indoctrination. During the 2004–5 school year, primary-school enrollment totaled 99.4 percent and secondary-school enrollment, 93.1 percent. In 2002–3 an estimated 192,000 students were enrolled in higher education. Workers attending university courses receive a state subsidy to provide for their dependents. Courses at intermediate and higher levels emphasize technology, agriculture, and teacher training. In 2002 budgetary expenditures on education represented 16.4 percent of total government spending. Education spending increased to more than 11 percent of gross domestic product (GDP) in 2004, up from 6.3 percent of GDP in 1998. By the 2004–5 educational year, there were 23 education professionals per 1,000 inhabitants, up from 20 in 2001–2.

Health: Cuba has a single, unified National Health System (Sistema Nacional de Salud—SNS). For the most part, the SNS is administered locally through an aggressive neighborhood health promotion program that makes heavy use of a network of easy-access institutions offering primary and secondary health-care services. At the national level, the Ministry of Public Health provides oversight. In 2004, 6.8 percent of Cuban medical facilities, including five hospitals and several dozen institutes, were subordinate to the Ministry of Public Health; most of Cuba's medical facilities (93.2 percent), including 279 hospitals, 436 polyclinics, and many other medical facilities, were subordinate to provincial and municipal administrative councils. The total amount spent on public health increased 59 percent between 1994 and 2000, an average annual increase of 9.6 percent. In 2004 Cuba spent a total of 6.2 percent of gross domestic product on health care. The total per capita expenditure on health at an average exchange rate in 2002 was US$197. In 2004 Cuba had 69,713 doctors, theoretically giving the country a ratio of about one doctor per 161 residents, as compared with one doctor per 188 residents in the United States; in theory, family doctors covered 99.4 percent of the population.

The health profile of the Cuban population is more like that of a developed country than a developing one, with low infant mortality, low fertility, low rates of infectious disease, and high cancer and cardiovascular disease rates. Despite Cuba's relatively meager resources, the primary health care system is still able to provide almost universal coverage and to ensure the continuance of low mortality among those less than 65 years of age even in the face of rising health threats. More than 95 percent of pregnant women receive prenatal care, and 98 to 99 percent of newborns are delivered in hospitals, factors that contribute to low infant and maternal mortality. Cuba also has high vaccination rates for childhood diseases, plus children up to age seven receive additional food rations through the ration card system.

The leading causes of death in 2000 were chronic noncommunicable diseases. Diseases of the heart, malignant neoplasms, and cerebrovascular diseases accounted for 60 percent of all deaths. In 2000 the most frequent communicable diseases were acute diarrheal diseases and acute respiratory infections. Dengue fever is also prevalent. Between 1986 and 2000, 3,231 individuals tested positive for human immunodeficiency virus (HIV)/acquired immune deficiency syndrome

(AIDS); 1,194 of these developed AIDS, and 840 died of the condition. Between 1995 and 2000, 839 cases of AIDS were reported, 50 percent of them in Havana; 76 percent of those affected were males. The HIV/AIDS prevalence rate among the adult population aged 15 to 49 in 2001 was 0.1 percent. The most frequent route of transmission is sexual (98 percent). All HIV-infected persons and AIDS patients receive treatment free of charge. The association of HIV infection with tuberculosis occurred in 7 percent of cases during 1986–99.

In 2000 mortality in urban areas was 755 per 100,000, 1.4 times greater than in rural areas. Reports suggest that accidents involving motor vehicles are the leading cause of accidental death in Cuba; many accidents involve motorists striking pedestrians or bicyclists. Suicide deaths were 16.4 per 100,000 population. Next to crime, lack of adequate housing is widely considered to be one of the two principal social problems affecting the health of Cubans. Overcrowding has greatly worsened during the past 15 years as a result of deteriorating housing conditions and lack of new housing construction, creating risks to both physical and mental health from stress and despair, as evidenced by a high suicide rate and emigration.

Despite the well-organized medical system and impressive health indicators, Cuba's overall medical capabilities are below U.S. standards. Cuban medical professionals are generally competent, but many health facilities face shortages of medical supplies and bed space. While the Cuban ruling elite and medical tourists enjoy high-quality medical care, medicines as common as aspirin are often unavailable to the general public. The Cuban government is trying to make the country self-sufficient in the production of pharmaceuticals. As of 2004, it claimed to produce 579 out of 804 basic drugs needed for the nation's welfare. Drug shortages are forcing the state heath care system to focus more on preventive medicine.

Moreover, despite Cuba's impressive physicians-per-population ratio many Cuban doctors have been working abroad on Cuban medical missions for significantly more official pay than they could earn in Cuba. Cuban doctors and nurses have long worked overseas in humanitarian missions. Over the last four decades, Cuba has loaned more than 52,000 medical workers to 95 countries in the developing world. Venezuela has been the primary destination for Cuban doctors since November 2001, when Cuba and Venezuela signed a barter agreement. By 2005 about 20,000 Cuban medical workers, including more than 14,000 doctors (approximately one-fifth of Cuba's doctors) were practicing in Venezuela in exchange for Venezuelan oil. A total of 30,000 Cuban health-care professionals were scheduled to be working in Venezuela in 2006–7. More than 1,000 Cuban medical workers also were serving in Bolivia (700), Haiti, and East Timor. With so many Cuban doctors serving abroad, the actual number of family doctors in Cuba was reported to be only 31,530. Consequently, Cubans increasingly complain that not enough doctors have remained in Cuba to take care of Cubans; they especially resent the absence of neighborhood physicians once provided free of charge.

Welfare: Despite the almost subsistence-level wages of most Cubans, they are generally much better off than citizens of many other developing countries because their meager salaries are supplemented with free education, subsidized medical care, housing, and some subsidized food. In terms of the Human Development Report's human poverty index (HPI), which focuses on the proportion of people below a threshold level in basic dimensions of human development—living a long and healthy life, having access to education, and a decent standard of living—Cuba ranked an impressive fifth in Latin America and the Caribbean in 2003.

Nevertheless, because government financial resources have contracted dramatically, the extensive and generous social safety net developed by socialist Cuba is currently incapable of providing the protection for which it was designed. Cuba can no longer afford to provide the extremely liberal social and economic benefits that, in addition to full employment, traditionally included generous social entitlements such as early retirement (at age 60 for men, 55 for women) and a broad array of partially or wholly subsidized social services, such as public transportation and meals in government-owned cafeterias. Demographic trends further aggravate the erosion of the safety net. With a rapidly aging population, the demands placed on the social safety net have multiplied as the number of elderly has increased.

As much as 99 percent of the population (or at least 95 percent of the urban population and 78 percent of the rural population) is reported to have access to safe water, one of the highest figures in Latin America. Cuba's potable water is derived primarily (72 percent) from underground sources. Of the water supplied, 94 percent receives treatment. In 2000 an estimated 38 percent of the population had access to sewerage systems and 55 percent to septic tanks and latrines. At the end of 2005, the country's water distribution and sanitation systems reportedly were in dire need of repair.

ECONOMY

Overview: Cuba has a state-controlled economy with the exception of a tiny and shrinking open-market sector. Since Fidel Castro seized power, a vast and cumbersome bureaucracy not conducive to innovation, productivity, and efficiency has managed Cuban affairs. Since its collapse in the 1990s following the abrupt withdrawal of Soviet funding, the Cuban economy has been recovering slowly and remains feeble. The sugar industry, traditionally the economy's mainstay, is in decline, and the country now relies more on the nickel and tourism industries, as well as a barter arrangement with Venezuela under which Cuba supplies doctors and teachers in exchange for crude oil and petroleum products at a discounted rate. In the absence of large amounts of capital and access to markets and in the face of continued U.S. trade sanctions, Cuba's economic situation is unlikely to improve substantially. During 2005, however, the surge in the availability of foreign exchange—as a result of new financing from China, trade agreements with Venezuela, and the continued strong growth of international tourism—enabled the government to increase state investment in projects such as repairing the critically dilapidated infrastructure and to increase wages and benefits.

In addition to the formal economy, Cuba has a large informal, or second, economy. Informal economic activities include agriculture, where private farmers control a portion of the land; the sale of certain personal services; and, beginning in the early 1990s, farmers' markets and artisan markets. Currently, about 300 farmers' markets reportedly operate in Cuba. Other economic activities outside of state control include illegal activities such as black-market operations and unauthorized use of government resources. For example, there are extensive informal markets in the exchange of homes, which are often secured by making illegal payments through intermediaries; and building materials often are stolen (mainly by insiders) from building projects or warehouses.

Gross Domestic Product (GDP): GDP per capita totaled US$3,224 in 2005, based on an estimated GDP of US$36.2 billion, and US$3,531 in 2006, based on a forecast GDP of US$39.7 billion. Real GDP, buoyed by expansion of services, especially in health and education, reached a record level in 2005. Using its official methodology, which differs from standard international measures by including public services at market value rather than cost, the Castro government estimated GDP growth for 2005 at 11.8 percent and forecast 10 percent growth for 2006. According to the standard definitions of GDP, however, real GDP growth totaled an estimated 4.2 percent in 2004 and 8 percent in 2005. A growth rate of about 6 percent has been forecast for 2006 and 10 percent for 2007. In 2005 the estimated origins of GDP were agriculture and fisheries, 5.4 percent; construction, 7.0 percent; electricity, gas, and water supply, 1.9 percent; manufacturing, 15.4 percent; mining, 1.4 percent; and services, 68.9 percent.

Government Budget: Cuba had large budget deficits throughout the 1990s. By 2002 the budget deficit totaled approximately US$1 billion. As a result of sharply increased government spending and income, the nominal fiscal deficit widened in 2005 to 4.8 percent of gross domestic product (GDP)—up from 4.2 percent in 2004. The fiscal deficit was expected to decline to just below 4 percent of GDP in 2006–7.

Inflation: Consumer price inflation in Cuba is determined by price fluctuations in both the domestic market of Cuban pesos (CuPs) and the official market of convertible pesos (CUCs), which are used in hard-currency retail outlets. Neither official nor unofficial exchange rates, which vary widely, are close to a purchasing power parity level, but the two domestic currencies reportedly are to be brought gradually into closer alignment by the end of 2007, by which time inflation is expected to moderate. Consumer price inflation averaged 1.3 percent in 2004 and 7.0 percent in 2005; estimates for 2006 and 2007 were for 5.9 percent and 5.0 percent, respectively.

Agriculture, Forestry, and Fishing: Agriculture and fisheries accounted for 5.4 percent of the gross domestic product (GDP) in 2005 and an expected 5.2 percent in 2006. After sugar output diminished dramatically during the 1990s, the restructuring of the sugar industry, formerly Cuba's leading industry, began in 2002. The crisis in the industry deepened with the 2004–5 sugar harvest (January–May), which was only 1.3 million tons (a record low) following a two-year drought, as compared with a 1990 level of 8 million tons. From gross agricultural production growth of 0.2 percent in 2004, the figure plummeted to –11.6 percent in 2005 but was expected to reach 3.8 percent in 2006 and 10 percent in 2007. The depressed agricultural output in 2005 was reflected in the sharp increase in import spending on agricultural goods that year (from US$1.2 billion in 2004 to more than US$1.5 billion in 2005), as well as in food-price increases in domestic agricultural markets. This situation appears to have given rise to a debate within the government itself about the fate of the sugar industry, some voicing concern about the government's decision announced in September 2005 to accelerate restructuring. As of April 2006 when international sugar prices were rising, Cuba was seeking foreign investment in the sugar industry for the first time and also planning to increase harvests.

As a result of a reforestation program, forests covered 21 percent of Cuban territory by the mid-1990s, as compared with only 18 percent in 1987. By 2005, the figure had reached 24 percent, and a new reforestation program was under way with a target of increasing coverage to 29 percent by 2015. The forestry programs expand the tree-covered area by 50,000 hectares each year. In comparison, the tree-covered area is expanded by less than 20,000 hectares per year when logging is used. Roundwood production in 2000 amounted to 3.3 million cubic meters and sawn wood to 146,000 cubic meters. Official Cuban figures show that the country's forests in 2006 held more than 130 million cubic meters of usable lumber and had the potential to grow 7.5 million cubic meters annually. However, reforestation in general has suffered from funding and other resource shortages since the 1990s.

Although Cuba's annual fish catch was approximately 130,000 tons before the economic crisis of the 1990s, the total dropped by about two-thirds between 1990 and 1994 as a result of a lack of investment, fuel, and operating capital, and the fishing industry has yet to recover. There had been some potential for making up part of the shortfall in the 1990s by developing fish farming. By 1998 the fisheries of Cuba's man-made reservoirs, totaling an estimated 148,000 hectares, had become the main source of fish for domestic consumers, with production totaling more than 70,000 tons, as compared with only 7,000 tons in 1980. By 2004, however, the output of fish farms and production (for export) of lobster and shrimp from coastal fisheries had shrunk to below the 1993 level (less than 20,000 tons), apparently as a result of an aging fishing fleet, increasingly expensive fuel, and fuel shortages.

Mining and Minerals: Mining accounted for 1.4 percent of the gross domestic product in 2005. Cuba is now the world's fifth-largest nickel and cobalt producer. Production of Cuba's primary mineral, nickel, was estimated to reach about 77,000 tons in 2005, an increase of more than 6 percent over 2004. The country's mineral resources are mined mostly by Canadian, Spanish, and other European companies.

Cuban oil production is currently limited to the coastal region in the northwest of the country. Cuba's crude is very heavy and has a high sulphur content. Nevertheless, high world oil prices have stimulated foreign interest in Cuban territorial waters in the Gulf of Mexico. In 1999 Cuba opened 112,000 square kilometers of its waters to foreign exploration. As of 2006, companies from Canada, China, India, Norway, and Spain have invested in drilling ventures in these waters.

Industry and Manufacturing: Industry in general accounted for about 25 percent of gross domestic product (GDP) in 2005 and was expected to increase slightly to 26.9 percent in 2006. Industrial production growth totaled 3.3 percent in 2004 and 5.1 percent in 2005 and was forecast to reach 13 percent in 2006 and 7.8 percent in 2007. Manufacturing accounted for 15.4 percent of GDP and construction for 7.0 percent in 2005. Power cuts and the contraction of sugar-related industries have hampered growth in the manufacturing sector except for a few industries, such as production of nickel and steel, neither of which is dependent on the electricity grid, and construction, which has benefited from the government's housing program and improvements to hospitals and schools. Growth in the construction sector reached 19 percent in 2005. The government's housing program that was approved in September 2005 envisaged the construction of 150,000 new homes by the end of 2006 and an additional 100,000 in 2007, representing the fastest pace of building since 1959. The actual totals may be somewhat lower.

Cuba currently has a national housing deficit of 500,000 units, especially in Havana, home to 2.8 million of Cuba's estimated 11.3 million people; 46 percent of Havana's 556,000 existing homes reportedly are in need of repairs.

Energy: Cuba depends primarily on petroleum to meet its modest energy requirements. Since the country's Soviet oil supply ended in the early 1990s, domestic oil production has increased significantly, but Cuba still relies on imported oil to meet its domestic needs. The price of these imports is therefore a major determinant of Cuba's terms of trade. Cuban petroleum production in 2005 was reportedly at least 65,000 barrels per day (bpd) of heavy crude with a high sulphur content, but possibly as much as 72,000 bpd (compared with only 16,000 bpd in 1984). Most of Cuba's oil production occurs in northern Matanzas Province, producing a heavy, sour crude that requires special processing at the country's refineries. Once remodeling work is completed on the Cienfuegos refinery in late 2007, the plan is to undertake a deep conversion project that will allow the Cuban refinery to double its capacity to refine Cuban and Venezuelan crude oil to 120,000 bpd. Almost all of Cuba's heavy crude oil production is used directly as boiler fuel in the electric power, cement, and nickel industries. Cuba has an annual deficit of approximately 100,000 bpd of crude oil/petroleum products in order to meet the minimum internal demand estimated to be around 170,000 bpd. Since reaching an agreement in November 2001, Venezuela has filled Cuba's petroleum-deficit requirement, supplying about half of Cuba's domestic oil consumption on preferential terms in exchange for medical and sports services.

Cuba consumes all of the natural gas that it produces (704 million cubic meters in 2004) and has no natural gas imports. The low volume of the country's rivers limits hydroelectric capacity. The country's 180 hydroelectric installations generate about 57 megawatts of electricity and mostly supply small rural communities.

In addition to having low generating capacity, the electricity sector has suffered from chronic system failures. Consumers experienced almost daily power cuts during the early 1990s. Despite some improvements in the second half of the decade, drastic action to reorganize and strengthen this sector was needed by mid-2004. Total electricity generation in 2005 declined by 2 percent. In a stopgap effort to ensure continuity of supply, the state electricity company spent about US$800 million in 2005 purchasing electric-power generating equipment from countries such as South Korea and Germany. In recent years, Cuba also has modernized and improved its electricity distribution network. As of mid-2006, newly installed electricity generation stations linked to the national grid had increased total national generation capacity by more than 1,000 MW, almost half of the generation needs for peak demand; by October 2006, capacity was planned to reach 1,400 MW. Nevertheless, in August 2006 a defect in the national electricity grid caused a major blackout in Havana and the provinces of Havana and Pinar del Río.

Services: In real terms, the services sector's output increased at an average rate of 4.4 percent per year during 1996–2002. Sectoral output increased by 2.4 percent in 2003 and by 10.8 percent in 2005. The services sector accounted for 68.9 percent of the gross domestic product in 2005. This share was expected to decline slightly to 67.9 percent in 2006. Receipts from tourism, a leading economic activity, totaled US$2.1 billion in 2004 and were expected to rise to US$2.6 billion in 2005. Agreements with Venezuela involving the employment of Cuban health care and education professionals in Venezuela and funding for medical treatment provided in Cuba for patients from Latin America and the Caribbean also account for the sharp rise in services earnings from around US$100 million in 1993 to US$3.1 billion in 2004 and approximately US$4.1 billion in 2005.

Banking and Finance: Since 1995 Cuba has been attempting to restructure its long nationalized banking system to accommodate a more market-oriented economy, hoping to attract foreign investment in the energy and mining sectors in particular. Relatively new commercial banks include the Banco Financiero Internacional and the Banco de Inversiones (for investment), Banco Metropolitano (offering foreign currency and deposit account facilities), Banco de Crédito y Comercio, Banco Internacional de Crédito, and Banco Nacional de Cuba. Cuba also has an older savings bank, the Banco Nacional de Ahorro, and 13 foreign banks (most of which are European). New rules issued since 2004 have enhanced the ability of the Central Bank of Cuba to monitor and control hard-currency credit creation in the country's monetary system. With the allocation of financial resources continuing to shift from the central planning authorities toward the banking system, the Central Bank is expected to play an increasingly important role in macroeconomic management, although the large informal economy's differing markets and divergent prices complicate monetary management. Cuba's financing requirement is expected to double in 2006 to about US$1 billion.

Labor: The labor force totaled at least 4.6 million people in 2004 and 4.7 million in 2005 but possibly as many as 6.7 million in both years and in 2006. Before the Revolution, women constituted less than 20 percent of the labor force. By the end of the century, however, that figure had risen to 44 percent, and the health sector alone employed 73.2 percent of women in the workforce. Although agriculture (including hunting, forestry, and fishing) employed 40 percent of the population in 1960, by 2002 it employed only about 26 percent of the economically active population. In 2002 the manufacturing industry employed 14 percent of the workforce (an increase of only 1 percent since 1960) and the services sector about 53 percent. Although the state sector accounted for 95.4 percent of total civilian employment in 1989, by 2003 this percentage had declined to 73.2 percent as a result of the economic reforms of the 1990s. About one-third of the employees in the state sector are engaged in providing community, social, and personal services, especially in health and education. The remainder of the labor force is made up mainly of private or cooperative farmers or the self-employed. Investment in universal education after 1959 has produced a well-educated workforce. Thus, it is a source of great frustration for many professionals that authorized self-employment opportunities are minimal; this category plus those employed by family businesses accounted for only 3.5 percent of the working population by 2003. The unemployment rate in 2004–5 was 1.9 percent, down from 3 percent in 2003, and was expected to remain at that level in 2006.

The minimum monthly wage varies by occupation; in 2005 it amounted to about US$9, allowing the typical worker and family to earn only enough for a minimal standard of living. Less than 1 percent of the labor force is occupied in much-coveted jobs in the new foreign sector. Foreign companies pay the government as much as US$500 to US$600 per worker per month, but workers receive only 5 percent of this amount because the government, which actually pays the wages of the Cuban workers employed by foreign companies, makes payments in Cuban pesos (CuP), which are not convertible to foreign currencies. Cuban state workers receive a portion of their wages in convertible pesos (CUC), but all other workers are paid only in Cuban pesos, even though many living expenses must be paid in convertible pesos.

Foreign Economic Relations: Prior to the Cuban Revolution, Cuba traded mostly with the United States. Since the United States imposed an economic embargo against the Castro regime in October 1960, U.S. trade sanctions against Cuba have remained in effect. From the early 1970s until the collapse of trade with the former Soviet bloc in 1990–91, more than 80 percent of Cuban trade was with Eastern Europe, mostly in nonconvertible-currency accounts (in effect, a barter arrangement). As Cuba sought to develop trade relations with the rest of the world after 1991, it began to conduct bilateral trade with Eastern Europe, including Russia, at world market prices. Although Cuba has signed some trade agreements with Russia since 2001, Cuban diplomatic efforts are more focused on deepening links with other potential trade partners such as China. The visit to Cuba of Chinese president Hu Jintao in November 2004 resulted in a set of trade agreements, including one to export 4,400 tons of nickel per year to China. China has been particularly interested in investing in Cuban infrastructure projects and in a major nickel mine in the east of the country. In 2005 China was Cuba's second most important trading partner (10 percent), mainly because of China's sugar imports.

The European Union (EU) accounts for about half of Cuba's external trade, and tourism from Europe has become an important currency earner, especially since Cuba began to accept the euro as exchange currency in 1999. Formal Cuban-EU relations remain cool, however, because by 1996 EU states had adopted a "common position" that is staunchly critical of the lack of progress on human rights and democratization in Cuba. The EU has prevented Cuba's accession to the Cotonou Accord, the mechanism through which it channels most developing country assistance and trade concessions. Nevertheless, the EU reopened diplomatic relations with Cuba in early 2005, acknowledging the ineffectiveness of EU sanctions imposed on Cuba in June 2003.

After Cuba lost support from the former Soviet bloc in 1990–91, the United States tightened economic sanctions against the island with the adoption in 1992 of the Torricelli Law. In 1996 the U.S. Congress passed the Libertad (Cuban Liberty and Democratic Solidarity) Act, also known as the Helms–Burton Law, which strengthened U.S. economic sanctions by threatening penalties for businesses known to have dealings with Cuba. After 1996 mounting pressure in the United States to relax sanctions led to some concessions, including permission for Cuban-Americans to send remittances of up to US$1,200 a year to relatives and, finally, in 2000 the legalization of food and medicine sales to Cuba beginning in January 2002. Under the George W. Bush administration, U.S. trade sanctions against Cuba intensified. On May 18, 2001, President Bush affirmed that his administration would "oppose any attempt to weaken sanctions against Cuba's government…until this regime frees its political prisoners, holds democratic, free elections, and allows for free speech."

Cuba's three most important regional trading partners are Canada, Mexico, and Venezuela—all three outspoken opponents of the U.S. economic embargo. In 2004 oil-rich Venezuela became Cuba's main source of imports (21.3 percent) but only its third most important export destination (10.2 percent). The bilateral trade is based on the oil-for-doctors program, which reportedly provides health coverage for 17 million Venezuelans in return for oil. Venezuela began paying Cuba in 2005 for the approximately 20,000 doctors and other health-care professionals working in Venezuela, as well as for the tens of thousands of eye surgeries and other medical operations that Cuban hospitals provide Venezuelans. As a result of the People's Trade Agreement signed

16

in Havana among Cuba, Bolivia, and Venezuela on April 29, 2006, Cuba will import Bolivian coca leaves for "legal consumption," as well as Bolivian soybeans and quinoa.

Cuba has actively participated in regional trade organizations not subject to a U.S. veto. It was a founding member of the Association of Caribbean States in 1995; joined the Latin American Integration Association in 1999 and the Caribbean Forum of African, Caribbean and Pacific States (Cariforum) as a full member in 2001; completed a trade and economic cooperation agreement with the Caribbean Community in 2002; belongs to the Caribbean Tourism Organization; and has indicated a desire to negotiate with the Common Market of the South (Mercado Común del Sur—Mercosur) and the Andean Community. Fidel Castro attended the Mercosur summit in Argentina in July 2006.

Imports: Cuba's imports dropped by 73 percent between 1990 and 1993 in the absence of export earnings and access to financing. However, import capacity, led by tourism revenue, has improved over the past decade. Imports of goods free on board totaled US$7 billion in 2005 and were projected to total US$7.9 billion in 2006 and US$8.5 billion in 2007. Principal imports in 2005 included foodstuffs (US$1.6 billion), fuels (US$1.8 billion), and machinery and equipment (US$1.7 billion). Other imported goods include chemicals (US$531 million in 2004).

In 2004 Venezuela was the leading source of imports, accounting for 21.3 percent of the total, followed by Spain (12 percent), China (11 percent), the United States (9.8 percent), Italy (5.1 percent), and Canada (4.9 percent). Estimated imports from Venezuela in 2005 totaled about US$1.4 billion, US$1.1 billion of which was oil (about 90,000 barrels per day) and US$300 million, food and other products. The estimate for 2006 was US$2 billion. Imports from China in 2005 also surged, to about US$560 million, making China Cuba's second-largest trading partner that year. After U.S. agricultural restrictions on exports to Cuba were partially lifted in 2001, one-way trade with the United States resumed in 2002 and totaled more than US$900 million during 2002–4 (no Cuban exports to the United States are allowed). However, the growth of this trade subsequently ended and began to decline after payment rules were tightened in early 2005.

Exports: Exports of goods free on board totaled US$2.7 billion in 2005 and were projected to total US$2.8 billion in 2006 and US$3.3 billion in 2007. Cuba's main exports in 2005 included nickel (US$1.2 billion), sugar and its by-products (US$168 million), and tobacco products (US$243 million). Other export products include medicines (US$130 million in 2004), seafood, citrus and tropical fruits, and coffee. Despite its decline, sugar remains an important export earner, second only to nickel as a commodity export, and is expected to earn about US$250 million in 2006. Although volume varies from year to year, Cuba's main export destinations in 2004 were the Netherlands (29.4 percent, a figure that includes goods shipped to the Netherlands for onward shipment to other European Union countries), Canada (22.4 percent), Venezuela (10.2 percent), Spain (8 percent), China (7.8 percent), and Russia (7.3 percent). Russia's purchases in 2004 represented a steady decline since 1999, when it purchased 22.2 percent of Cuba's exports.

Trade Balance: Trade figures for 2005–7 project continuing deficits in goods trading: US$4.3 billion in 2005, US$5.1 billion in 2006, and US$5.2 billion in 2007. However, the services balance improved from close to zero in 1990 to an estimated surplus of US$2.6 billion in 2005 and a projected surplus of US$2.8 billion in 2006. Tourism and the provision of health-care services to Venezuela account for most of the increase in services earnings.

Balance of Payments: Until 1990 the Soviet trading bloc, the Council for Mutual Economic Assistance (CMEA), financed Cuba's current account deficit. During 1992–2003, Cuba's restricted access to international capital kept the country's current account deficit under 2 percent of gross domestic product (GDP). After deficits in the current account of US$653 million in 2001, US$276 million in 2002, and US$136 million in 2003, the country's balance of payments enjoyed a surplus of US$134 million in 2004 and US$143 million in 2005, or about 0.2 percent of GDP in 2004 and 0.1 percent in 2005. The positive current account balance in 2004–5 was due primarily to Cuba's almost regular annual surpluses in the services balance, mainly as a result of strong revenues from international tourism and other services (such as health and education services exported to Venezuela in exchange for cheap oil), as well as new sources of financing from China and high nickel prices. The current account deficit was expected to be a relatively low US$374 million in 2006 (0.9 percent of GDP) and US$358 million in 2007 (0.8 percent of GDP).

On the capital account ledger, long-term capital (net) in 2004 totaled US$462 million; net direct investments, US$200 million; net other long-term capital inflows, US$670 million; other capital, US$922 million; and variation in reserves, –US$1.5 million. The country's estimated hard-currency international reserves reached US$2.1 billion in 2004, US$2.2 billion in 2005, and an estimated US$2.4 billion in 2006. The increase since 2003, when reserves totaled only US$638 million, has been attributed in part to Fidel Castro's ban in November 2004 on the use of U.S. dollars on the island.

External Debt: Although it still owes the Russian Federation more than US$20 billion, Cuba reportedly has agreed to make repayments in the form of goods, such as fuel and sugar. It remains unconfirmed how much external hard-currency debt grew in 2004, but the increase was about US$500 million according to one estimate. In 2005 the island's hard-currency debt, on which Cuba defaulted in 1986, was owed mainly to European and Latin American governments and totaled about US$12.5 billion, or approximately 35 percent of gross domestic product (GDP). External debt was expected to reach US$13.2 billion in 2006. Debt service in 2005 amounted to just over US$1 billion, and the due debt-service ratio was 13.9 percent. Official debt is almost all bilateral, such as with Japanese and European creditors, because Cuba has no access to the major multilateral financial institutions.

Foreign Investment: Under Cuba's 1995 Foreign Investment Act, all sectors are open to foreign capital except defense, public health care, and education. Foreign investors can freely repatriate profits and dividends. U.S. investors are barred from Cuba by U.S. legislation. The unresolved issue of U.S. property claims also has deterred investors from other countries. Most foreign investments to date have been in nickel mining, oil, tourism, and telecommunications. Net direct foreign investment flows totaled US$200 million in 2004 and US$500 million in 2005 and a projected US$620 million in 2006 and US$630 million in 2007. Major new trade agreements, investment commitments, and credit lines from China and Venezuela provided a significant boost in 2005 and were expected to continue to do so in 2006–7.

Foreign Aid: During the 1960–90 period, socialist countries provided nearly all of the substantial development financing received by Cuba. Originating primarily from the former Soviet Union and amounting to more than US$65 billion, the aid covered a wide range of economic activities, mostly taking the form of loans repayable at very low interest rates. Approximately 40 percent of the flow of resources (about US$25.7 billion) took the form of repayable loans (development credits, 13 percent; and credits to finance trade deficits, 27 percent); nonrepayable price subsidies accounted for the remaining 60 percent (US$39.4 billion). Cuba receives little multilateral agency development assistance because it is barred from membership in the World Bank, the International Monetary Fund, and the Inter-American Development Bank. Its main sources of multilateral assistance are European Union emergency relief and United Nations agencies, such as the World Food Programme, the United Nations Development Programme, the United Nations Regular Programme of Technical Assistance, and the United Nations Children's Fund. The Organization of the Petroleum Exporting Countries has cofinanced a development loan for the energy sector. In recent years, Latin American countries such as Venezuela also have provided some aid. Total multilateral aid amounted to only about US$20 million in 2004, whereas bilateral aid totaled US$69 million that year.

Currency and Exchange Rate: Cuban currency has no official value outside the country. Cuba has two domestic official currencies in circulation: the Cuban peso (CuP) and the convertible peso (CUC), both of which are equivalent to 100 centavos. As of November 8, 2004, Cuban authorities eliminated the circulation of U.S. dollars and any other "convertible currency" in the country, at least officially. Tourists and foreign business visitors are required to exchange their currency into convertible pesos on arrival because the Cuban government now requires the use of convertible pesos for all transactions other than the most basic street-vendor-type purchases, for which the Cuban peso is used. Retail stores that had been selling goods in U.S. dollars now can accept only convertible pesos, which are considered the equivalent of tourist dollars. The convertible peso is used for luxury products available in tourist boutiques known as "dollar shops" or for tourist-related services. In addition, Cubans must use convertible pesos to pay rents or make major purchases, even though most workers are paid in Cuban pesos rather than convertible pesos. As of September 27, 2006, the exchange rates for the two Cuban currencies were: US$1=22.22 Cuban pesos (floating domestic rate); and US$1=CUC0.93 (a fixed rate). The exchange of U.S. dollars for convertible pesos also bears a 10 percent tax that is not applied to other foreign currencies.

Fiscal Year: Cuba's fiscal year coincides with the calendar year.

TRANSPORTATION AND TELECOMMUNICATIONS

Overview: Cuba's transportation infrastructure consists of an integrated network of roads, railroads, airfields, ports, and inland waterways. Cuba has good transportation facilities and networks in the western and central portions of the island; the eastern portion of the island is less developed. Roads, railroads, and air and maritime transportation services provide access to almost every location on the island. The infrastructure of ports, airports, and warehouses supports extensive foreign trade. Land transportation has been severely affected by the economic crisis. Lack of spare parts for the bus and truck fleet has reduced significantly the number of vehicles in operation. Moreover, fuel shortages have forced cutbacks in the number of routes and their frequency. Transportation bottlenecks have affected labor productivity because workers are unable to get to their jobs on time or have to spend an inordinately long period of time commuting to their jobs.

Roads: By 2000 Cuba had an estimated 112,998 kilometers of roads, including at least 26,000 kilometers of paved roads (but more likely 29,820) and about 84,000 kilometers of unpaved roads, constituting one of the most developed road systems in the Caribbean. For five decades, the main highway was the Central Highway, mostly a two-lane road running for 1,200 kilometers from Pinar del Río in the west to Santiago de Cuba in the east. In the late 1970s, construction began on a new eight-lane National Expressway (commonly known as "Ocho Vías," or Eight Lanes), which was supposed to run the length of Cuba from Pinar del Río to Santiago de Cuba. However, the Ocho Vías, which lacks lights and is variously reported as in poor to good condition, extends only two-thirds of the way from Havana to the eastern tip of the island; moreover, washed-out sections and giant potholes limit traveling speeds. In addition, the Vía Blanca links Havana with Varadero, and the Vía Mulata links Baracoa and Santiago de Cuba in Cuba's southeast with the rest of the island. Although the main highways of Havana are generally well maintained, secondary streets usually are not.

Railroads: Despite being much more energy efficient than truck transport, particularly in transporting sugarcane or ore, railroad transportation has been neglected since 1959 in favor of truck transport. Although half of the rolling stock is in a dilapidated state, the country has an extensive rail network running the length of the island and connecting the large urban areas, industrial centers, and major and secondary ports, either directly or through branches. In 2004 the rail network for transporting passengers and general freight included 4,226 kilometers of 1.435-meter standard-gauge track and about 150 kilometers of electrified 0.914-meter narrow-gauge track. In addition, the island's sugar factories and plantations were served in 2004 by 7,742 kilometers of private track, about 65 percent standard gauge and the rest narrow gauge. The total volume of rail transport reportedly increased by 13 percent in 2005 with the aid of trade and agreements with China that allowed for repair of locomotives and purchases of new equipment.

Ports and Shipping: Cuba's ports are in generally good condition but in need of modernization and dredging. Cuba has 11 main ports capable of handling general export and import cargoes, including major deep-water ports at Cienfuegos, Havana, Mariel (the Free Trade Zone), Matanzas, Nipe, Nuevitas, and Santiago de Cuba. In addition, Cuba has eight bulk sugar-loading terminals and several other smaller import facilities, as well as specialized port facilities for the fishing fleet. Of the country's most used ports (Cienfuegos, Havana, Mariel, Matanzas, and Santiago de Cuba), Havana is the country's largest and most frequently accessed, with three main general cargo facilities that handle container vessels and roll-on/off vessels. During the 1990s, a new pier for cruise ships was built, and in 2001 various cruise ships from British, Canadian, Italian, and Spanish companies began to make Havana a port of call. Number one in sugar exports, the port of Cienfuegos is capable of handling one-third of Cuba's sugar production through its bulk sugar terminal. Its pier for handling oil and oil byproducts allows the berthing of ships up to 50,000 tons. Matanzas, located on the north coast, has a supertanker terminal with an oil pipeline that crosses to the Cienfuegos refinery on the south coast. The Cuban Mercantile Marine consists of 18 ships (of 1,000 tons or more) with a total tonnage of 89,091.

Inland Waterways: Cuba has 240 kilometers of navigable inland waterways, most of which are near the mouths of rivers.

Civil Aviation and Airports: In part because of the fast-growing tourism industry, Cuba has made considerable investments in upgrading and expanding its well-developed air transport infrastructure since the late 1990s. Ten of the civilian airports can now handle international flights, and nine of them are linked to the nine largest tourist resorts. Of Cuba's 170 airports in 2005, 78 had paved runways and 92, unpaved. Cuba's main international airports include Camagüey, Ciego de Ávila, Cienfuegos, Havana, Matanzas, Santiago de Cuba, and Varadero. Inaugurated in mid-1998, the new terminal at Havana's José Martí International Airport expanded the airport's capacity to 3 million people per year. The main national airports that handle primarily domestic flights include Baracoa, Bayamo, Cayo Largo, Guantánamo, Holguín, Manzanillo, Moa, Nicaro, Nueva Gerona, and Santa Clara.

The Cuban Aviation Company (Cubana de Aviación—Cubana) moves about half of the international tourists into Cuba and manages all of the main civilian airports. In addition to a comprehensive domestic service, Cubana operates—with the help of Canadian and Irish pilots—international services to various regional and international destinations. Latin American, Canadian, Czech, German, Mexican, Russian, and Spanish airlines also serve Cuba.

Pipelines: In 2004 Cuba's gas pipelines totaled 49 kilometers and its oil pipelines 230 kilometers.

Telecommunications: Most of the telecommunications infrastructure dates to the period before the 1959 Revolution and uses technology that has outlived its life cycle many times over. Newer facilities were installed during the 1990s with the assistance of foreign telecommunications services partners. A Cuban-Italian joint venture completed work on a national fiber-optic system in 2004, and 85 percent of its switches were already digitized by the end of the year. Nevertheless, telephone line density remains low, at 10 per 100 inhabitants. By 2004 Cuba had 844,000 telephone subscribers, or 7.45 per 100 inhabitants, according to the Geneva-based International Telecommunication Union. According to the official Cuban Web site, however, the country had only 520,865 main telephone lines, or 4.7 telephone lines per 100 inhabitants, with a 41 percent call-completion rate. Approximately 45 percent of Cuba's telephone lines serve residents within Havana's metropolitan area.

Cuba's national infrastructure supports national and international telecommunications services utilizing wired and wireless facilities. Teléfonos Celulares de Cuba, S.A. (Cubacel) provides mobile telephone coverage around most towns. Initially, the main subscribers, numbering 2,900 in 2001, were mostly government officials, diplomats, and company employees in the Havana area. However, during 1999–2004 cellular phone subscribers increased by 71.3 percent, reaching a rate of 0.67 per 100 inhabitants in 2004 and accounting for 9 percent of total telephone subscribers. By the end of 2005, Cuba had 80,000 mobile subscribers.

A relatively small proportion of the Cuban population has access to the Internet, since the cost is prohibitive for most Cubans. Those who do have Internet access are mostly people with institutional e-mail accounts, diplomats, or foreign businesspeople. In 2004 Cuba had 1,712 Internet hosts (1.51 per 10,000 inhabitants) and about 150,000 Internet users (only 1.32 users per 100 inhabitants). The number of personal computers (PCs) totaled about 420,000 in 2005, or 3.7 per 100 inhabitants; another 200,000 PCs were expected to be in use in 2006. Cuba's Internet usage figures reflect a growth of 150 percent during 2000–5. Presently, Cuba accounts for 3.5 percent of Internet users in Latin America.

GOVERNMENT AND POLITICS

Overview: Since 1965 Cuba has been governed by a highly centralized system headed by the Communist Party of Cuba (Partido Comunista de Cuba—PCC), which is the only authorized political party and rules as "the highest leading force of society and the State," according to the constitution. The Council of State of the National Assembly of Popular Power is the state's highest decision-making body, and the Council of Ministers is the highest executive and administrative authority. Beginning on December 2, 1976, Castro assumed the functions of president of the Council of State and Council of Ministers. A People's Supreme Court, accountable to the National Assembly, oversees a system of regional courts. Municipal, regional, and provincial assemblies also have been established.

On July 31, 2006, Cuban news media reported an official "proclamation" that Fidel Castro, the long-time chief of state and head of government as president of the Council of State and Council of Ministers, first secretary of the Political Bureau of the Central Committee of the PCC, and commander in chief of the Revolutionary Armed Forces (Fuerzas Armadas Revolucionarias—FAR), had undergone emergency intestinal surgery and consequently had transferred power and all of his principal government and party positions provisionally—for the first time in his 47-year rule—to his brother and long-time designated successor, Raúl Castro. Raúl Castro already had been serving equally as long as minister of the FAR, first vice president of the Council of State and Council of Ministers, and second secretary of the PCC's Political Bureau.

In addition, Fidel Castro transferred his functions as principal coordinator of the National and International Program of Public Health to José Ramón Balaguer Cabrera, a member of the Political Bureau and minister of public health; his functions as principal coordinator of the National and International Education Program to two Political Bureau members, José Ramón Machado Ventura and Esteban Lazo Hernández; and his functions as principal coordinator of the National Program of the Energy Revolution in Cuba to Carlos Lage Dávila, a member of the Political Bureau and secretary of the Executive Committee of the Council of Ministers. Fidel Castro also transferred his personal control of funding for these health, education, and energy programs to a funding committee consisting of Lage Dávila; Francisco Soberón Valdés, minister-president of the Central Bank of Cuba; and Felipe Pérez Roque, minister of foreign relations.

On August 13, on the occasion of Fidel Castro's eightieth birthday and a visit by Venezuelan President Hugo Chávez Frías, Raúl Castro made his first public appearance as provisional president by greeting Chávez at the Havana airport. The following day, the electronic version of

Granma, the official communist party newspaper, published photos of Castro being visited in his hospital room on his birthday by his brother and President Chávez. Despite Castro's apparent improvement, in late September there was no indication that he would be resuming the full roster of his previous powers anytime soon, if at all. The temporary transfer of power, described by some observers as a dress rehearsal for a post-Castro transition, appeared more likely to become the actual succession. Nor was there any clear evidence that the leadership transition would evolve toward democratization, despite the assertion of opposition leader Osvaldo José Payá Sadinas that *fidelismo* would not survive Fidel and that Raúl Castro's assumption of power would mean the country had entered a stage of substantial democratic opening. In the shorter term, according to some outside experts, a likely scenario is for Raúl Castro to serve as a pragmatic but low-profile chairman of a collective leadership until elections are held for the Council of State president and first secretary of the PCC.

Likely key leaders include the aforementioned younger-generation leaders, but particularly Lage Dávila and Pérez Roque, along with National Assembly President Ricardo Alarcón de Quesada, who is Cuba's most experienced diplomat. Although Raúl Castro apparently retains strong support within the FAR for his competent management of one of Cuba's strongest institutions as well as for his successful command of the FAR during three overseas wars, his leadership of a post–Fidel Castro administration would itself likely be transitional because of his age—he turned 75 on June 3, 2006, reportedly poor health, and lack of his brother's charisma and national and international stature. Interior Minister and Army Corps General Abelardo Colomé Ibarra, who is next in the hierarchy of power after Raúl Castro, would be another likely transitional candidate; as a revolutionary comrade of the Castro brothers, Colomé would likely advocate a continued strong military role in government.

Executive Branch: The 31-member Council of State, whose members and president are elected by the National Assembly of Popular Power to serve as the Assembly's permanent organ, is, in effect, the highest decision-making representative of the state because the National Assembly meets only twice a year for a few days each time. The president of the Council of State is also president of the Council of Ministers, in which executive and administrative authority is vested, and thus serves as both chief of state and head of government. In mid-2006, the Council of Ministers had 28 ministry posts (two of which were vacant), including the minister without portfolio. The constitution empowers the Council of Ministers, as the highest executive and administrative organ, to issue regulations to administer laws and decrees and to authorize exceptions to state ownership of the means of production. The ministers are responsible principally to the Council's nine-member Executive Committee, which includes its president, first vice president, and five other vice presidents. The Executive Committee is the decision-making body of the Council of Ministers, and one of its main functions is to oversee the administration of the economy. The Council of Ministers answers to the National Assembly and to the Council of State. The president and vice presidents of the Council of State and the National Assembly elect ministers for a term of five years. Elections were last held in March 2003 and are next scheduled for 2008.

The 24-member Political Bureau of the Central Committee of the Communist Party of Cuba (Partido Comunista de Cuba—PCC) is the party's leading decision-making institution and Cuba's most important decision-making entity. The PCC monopolizes all government positions, including judicial offices, and approves candidates for any elected office. The PCC's highest authority is the Party Congress, which elects a Central Committee (150 members in 2005) to supervise the party's work. To direct its policy, the Central Committee elects a Politburo (24 members in 2005).

Legislative Branch: As amended in July 1992, the 1976 constitution vests all formal legislative powers (including the powers to amend the constitution) in the National Assembly of Popular Power (Asamblea Nacional de Poder Popular—ANPP). The National Assembly is the supreme organ of state and the sole legislative authority. Prior to 1976, the Council of Ministers had exercised both executive and legislative functions. The National Assembly elects 31 of its members to form the Council of State, the Assembly's permanent organ. The National Assembly has the formal power, among others, to approve the budget and the national economic plan; elect the members of the Supreme Court; and generally oversee the rule-making activities and electoral processes of the provincial assemblies and municipal assemblies. The 609 National Assembly deputies are elected by direct popular vote for five-year terms.

Judicial Branch: The constitution explicitly subordinates the judiciary to the National Assembly and the Council of State. The Cuban court system consists of a People's Supreme Court, provincial courts, municipal courts, and military courts. The People's Supreme Court, the highest judicial body, is organized into five chambers: criminal, civil and administrative, labor, state security, and military. Its members are nominated by the minister of justice and confirmed by the National Assembly with two exceptions: First, its president and vice president are nominated by the president of the Council of State; second, the members of the military chamber are nominated jointly by the minister of justice and the minister of the Revolutionary Armed Forces. The minister of justice exercises administrative control over all the courts, including the People's Supreme Court, which has no authority to declare a law unconstitutional. Judges are appointed for a term, not for life, and they can be removed from office if proper cause is shown. As a result, the courts show considerable deference to executive authority and are marked by political timidity. The Office of the State Prosecutor is subordinate to the National Assembly, which formally elects the prosecutor. This office has wide latitude to review the past conduct and prospective actions of all organs of state power. The prosecutor has specific oversight over all law enforcement and a rank equal to a Supreme Court justice. The prosecutor is directly responsible for cases of treason or corruption.

Administrative Divisions: In 1976 the Council of Ministers divided Cuba into 14 provinces and 169 municipalities. Listed from west to east, Cuba's provinces are Pinar del Río, La Habana, Ciudad de La Habana, Matanzas, Villa Clara, Cienfuegos, Sancti Spíritus, Ciego de Ávila, Camagüey, Las Tunas, Granma, Holguín, Santiago de Cuba, and Guantánamo. The Isla de la Juventud (Isle of Youth), the Cuban archipelago's second-largest island, is a special municipality.

Provincial and Local Government: The central government directly oversees the provincial and local governments through a hierarchical network of assemblies and committees. Each of Cuba's 14 provinces is formally governed by a provincial assembly, which elects a provincial committee. The president of the provincial committee functions as the provincial governor. A provincial assembly must have at least 75 members, and they serve for five years. Each of the country's 169 municipalities is governed by a municipal assembly, which elects a municipal committee, whose president functions as mayor. Municipal assembly delegates serve for two and one-half years. Nominations for municipal assembly elections come from regional assemblies at the precinct level.

Judicial and Legal System: A civil law state, Cuba has a legal system that is based on Spanish and American law but influenced by communist legal theory. Cuba's inquisitorial system of criminal procedure emphasizes written codes rather than precedent as the source of law. There are no jury trials, and most trials are public. The courts are key institutions in law enforcement and also seek to educate the population about their rights and obligations. The provincial courts exercise jurisdiction over crimes for which punishment will not exceed eight years; about three-quarters of all crimes fall within their realm. Municipal courts serve as trial courts at the lowest level, and they have jurisdiction over minor crimes that typically carry a penalty of imprisonment for less than one year or small fines. They are also the courts of first instance in civil and labor cases. Municipal trials are always held before a panel of three judges. All of Cuba's courts have both professional and lay judges. Professional judges are selected through a competitive examination administered by the Ministry of Justice. About half of Cuba's judges are members of the Cuban Communist Party, and an even higher proportion of party members is evident in the Supreme Court. Cuban courts are very harsh in their treatment of the political opposition. Cubans can be jailed for speaking ill of their rulers or for organizing groups to contest political power.

Electoral System: Elections for the National Assembly are held in multimember districts. Voters have three choices: vote for the single official slate, vote for some of the candidates on the official slate (but never for opposition party candidates), or cast a blank ballot. To be elected, a candidate has to receive more than half of the valid votes cast. Elections to the National Assembly take place every five years. No candidate failed to be elected in the 1993 and 1998 National Assembly elections. The last elections for the National Assembly and provincial assemblies were held in January 2003; the next elections are slated for January 2008. Municipal elections were last held in April 2005 and are next due in October 2007.

Political Parties and Politics: The Cuban Communist Party (Partido Comunista de Cuba— PCC) has governed Cuba since 1965. The PCC is the only legal political party and exercises de facto control over government policies. Major issues are debated at periodic party congresses, the fifth of which was held in October 1997. These congresses adopt the party's statutes and programs and choose the membership of the Central Committee and Political Bureau. Key issues are discussed more regularly in meetings of the Political Bureau, which includes Cuba's most powerful leaders. The Central Committee, a much larger entity, meets annually and includes many key intermediate-level leaders.

Mass Media: In the absence of any freedoms of speech and press, domestic media must operate under party guidelines and reflect government views. The state owns and operates all mass media except for publications of the Roman Catholic Church. The Cuban government and Communist Party of Cuba (Partido Comunista de Cuba—PCC) strictly censor news, information, and commentary and restrict dissemination of foreign publications to tourist hotels. Laws against disseminating antigovernment propaganda, graffiti, and disrespect of officials carry prison penalties.

Cuba has several dozen online regional newspapers. The only national daily paper is *Granma*, the official organ of the PCC. A weekly version, *Granma International*, is published in English, Spanish, French, Portuguese, and German plus is available online. Havana residents also have their own weekly, Havana-oriented paper, *Tribuna de La Habana*. The weekly *Juventud Rebelde* is the official organ of the Communist Youth Union. The biweekly *Bohemia* is the country's only general-interest newsmagazine. Cuba's official news agency is Prensa Latina, which publishes several magazines, including *Cuba Internacional*, directed at the foreign audience.

In 2005 Cubans had at least 3.9 million radio receivers and 3 million television sets, and the country had 169 AM, 55 FM, and 58 TV broadcasting stations. The Cuban Institute of Radio and Television serves as the government's administrative outlet for broadcasting. Of the six national FM radio stations, the top three are Radio Progreso, Radio Reloj, and Radio Rebelde, in that order. Two other national radio networks that also provide news and entertainment are Radio Musical Nacional (CMBF) and Radio Enciclopedia. Another station, Radio Taíno, promotes tourism. The Cuban government also operates Radio Havana, the official Cuban international short-wave radio service. The Cuban television system is made up of two networks: Cubavisión and Tele Rebelde. Cuba's restriction of foreign broadcast media is one reason the U.S. government has sponsored radio and television broadcasting into Cuba through Radio and TV Martí, much of which is jammed.

Internet access is restricted by prohibitive cost, by very limited accessibility, by the relatively small (albeit rapidly expanding) number of personal computers, and by government efforts to control information access. Local post offices provide public access to e-mail, but many facilities do not provide international access. Access to the World Wide Web is mainly restricted to government offices, research and educational institutes, and large companies.

Foreign Relations: With the demise of the Soviet Union and the end of the Cold War, Cuba ended its long-time efforts to export Marxist revolution and adopted a pragmatic foreign policy that is designed to expand Cuba's international relations and trade, as well as tourism and investment in Cuba. Cuba is no longer the major diplomatic player in the developing world that it was during the Cold War, when it was able to send troops to support revolutionary movements or regimes. Nevertheless, it still has the largest diplomatic representation of any Latin American country: 177 embassies and three consulates worldwide, and it continues to play an active role in its relations with the developing world, serving as host for the Non-Aligned Movement (NAM) Summit on September 11–16, 2006, and taking over chairmanship of the NAM from Malaysia. Cuban relations with Russia remain cautious. Cuba's diplomatic efforts are more focused on deepening links with major trade partners, namely China and Venezuela. Cuba also has sought closer ties with Vietnam and North Korea. As its trade ties with China and Venezuela have increased, Cuba has shown declining interest in wooing the European Union (EU), which, despite being an outspoken critic of the U.S. embargo on Cuba, is divided about cooperating with Cuba because of the island's poor human rights record and lack of democracy. Cuba has continued to cultivate relations with individual EU member countries.

In the Americas, Cuba has used the election of a series of left-leaning presidents in countries such as Brazil, Bolivia, and Venezuela to develop relations with those countries and the region in general. Cuba also has continued to foster close political and commercial ties with Mexico and

Canada, both of which have been strong critics of the U.S. economic embargo. However, diplomatic relations between Cuba and Mexico have been strained since 2001 over Cuba's human rights record and reached their lowest point in more than a century in April 2004, when Mexico voted against Cuba for the third time at the United Nations Human Rights Commission. Mexico sent a new ambassador to Cuba in September 2005 after seven months without diplomatic representation. Cuba's relations with its Caribbean neighbors have improved slowly since 1991, and Fidel Castro has made several state visits throughout the Caribbean region. Relations between Jamaica and Cuba, which have direct air links, are now fairly good.

Cuba and the United States have not had formal diplomatic relations since 1961, but each country maintains an Interests Section in the other's capital. Bilateral Cuban-U.S. relations have remained highly antagonistic since the communist government of Fidel Castro came to power. Progress in this area has been severely constrained by the enduring rigidities of the communist regime and the inflexible U.S. policy stance. The U.S. government has sought to further tighten the implementation of economic sanctions, despite lack of congressional support for such a move. In a rare instance of Cuban-U.S. collaboration, Cuban and U.S. doctors worked together for the first time in May 2005 during a seven-day visit to Honduras by a Cuban Medical Brigade. Prospects for an improvement in Cuban-U.S. relations and lifting of the Cold War–era U.S. trade embargo remain poor until the Castro era ends, the country opens to democratization, and the politically powerful émigré community in the United States drops its traditional opposition to any rapprochement.

Membership in International Organizations: Cuba is excluded from hemispheric organizations subject to the U.S. veto, including the Americas Summit, the Organization of American States, the Inter-American Development Bank, and negotiations over the Free-Trade Area of the Americas. Cuba has been accepted as a full member of the African, Caribbean, and Pacific (ACP) group of countries associated with the European Union (EU), although it is not a beneficiary of ACP–EU trade agreements. Cuba is a member of all United Nations (UN) agencies, including the regional body and the UN Economic Commission for Latin America and the Caribbean. Cuba is also a member of the Customs Co-operation Council, Food and Agriculture Organization, Group of 77, International Atomic Energy Agency, International Civil Aviation Organization, International Criminal Police Organization, International Fund for Agricultural Development, International Hydrographic Organization, International Labour Organisation, International Maritime Organization, International Maritime Satellite Organization, International Red Cross and Red Crescent Movement, International Olympic Committee, International Organization for Standardization, International Telecommunication Union, International Telecommunications Satellite Organization (nonsignatory user), Latin American Economic System, Non-Aligned Movement, Permanent Court of Arbitration, Universal Postal Union, World Confederation of Labor, World Federation of Trade Unions, World Health Organization, World Intellectual Property Organization, World Meteorological Organization, World Tourism Organization, and World Trade Organization.

Major International Treaties: In the area of counternarcotics, Cuba is a party to the 1988 United Nations Drug Convention, the 1971 United Nations Convention on Psychotropic Substances, and the 1961 United Nations Single Convention on Narcotic Drugs, as amended by the 1972 Protocol. The Cuban government has not signed the Agreement Concerning Cooperation in Suppressing Illicit Maritime and Air Trafficking in Narcotic Drugs and Psychotropic Substances in the Caribbean Area (Caribbean Regional Maritime Agreement), despite its participation in the agreement negotiations. Cuba has signed, but not ratified, the United Nations Convention against Transnational Organized Crime. Cuba maintains bilateral narcotics agreements with 33 countries and less formal agreements with 16 others.

Cuba is a signatory of the following environmental treaties or protocols, among others: Antarctic, Convention for the Protection and Development of the Marine Environment of the Wider Caribbean Region, Convention on Biological Diversity, Convention on Nature Protection and Wildlife Preservation in the Western Hemisphere, Desertification, Development of the Marine Environment of the Wider Caribbean Region, Endangered Species, Environmental Modification, Hazardous Wastes, Marine Dumping, Ozone Layer Protection, Ship Pollution, and United Nations Convention on the Law of the Sea. It has signed but not ratified the Protocol on Environmental Protection to the Antarctic Treaty, the Convention on Climate Change and Kyoto Protocol, and Marine Life Conservation.

In 1995 Cuba signed the Treaty for the Prohibition of Nuclear Weapons in Latin America and the Caribbean (Treaty of Tlatelolco), a Latin American regional nonproliferation regime, but declined to ratify the treaty and bring it into force until October 2002. Cuba submitted its ratification of the Nuclear Non-Proliferation Treaty (NPT) in November 2002.

NATIONAL SECURITY

Armed Forces Overview: The Revolutionary Armed Forces (Fuerzas Armadas Revolucionarias—FAR) was one of the largest and most formidable militaries in the Latin American region if not in the entire developing world in the mid-1980s, when it still received substantial Soviet aid, but it declined greatly during the post-Soviet years of the 1990s. It remains the most powerful military force in the Caribbean area. Numbering an estimated 49,000 active members in 2006, the FAR consists of the 38,000-member Revolutionary Army (Ejército Revolucionario), the 3,000-member (including 500 marines) Revolutionary Navy (Marina de Guerra Revolucionaria—MGR), and the 8,000-member Antiaircraft Defense and Revolutionary Air Force (Defensa Antiaérea y Fuerza Aérea Revolucionaria—DAAFAR). In addition, the FAR has 39,000 reservists. Today the FAR has a primarily defensive and deterrent orientation. The army remains both well equipped and professional and is one of the strongest defensive military forces in Latin America, capable of offering strong resistance to an invading power. Traditionally a well-trained and professional force, the DAAFAR has been hobbled by a chronic lack of fuel and replacement parts and as a result has continued to decline in effectiveness. The MGR has been reduced to basically a coast guard.

The Ministry of the Revolutionary Armed Forces (Ministerio de las Fuerzas Armadas Revolucionarias—MINFAR) commands the FAR. As president of the Council of State and Council of Ministers, General Fidel Castro Ruz had been commander in chief of the FAR, until July 31, 2006, when, for health reasons, he provisionally transferred these functions to his brother, Raúl Castro Ruz, who is also minister for the FAR and chief of the Joint General Staff. The army, navy, and air force each have a general staff under the control of the Joint General

Staff. The Cuban military is divided into three major geographical commands: Western (headquartered in Havana), covering the capital and the provinces of Ciudad de La Habana and Pinar del Río; Central (headquartered in Matanzas), covering the provinces of Matanzas, Villa Clara, Cienfuegos, and Sancti Spíritus; and Eastern (headquartered in Santiago de Cuba), covering the provinces of Santiago de Cuba, Guantánamo, Granma, Holguín, Las Tunas, Camagüey, and Ciego de Ávila. Each of the three regional army commands and the Isle of Youth Autonomous Military Region has its own staff organization and reports to Raúl Castro.

Foreign Military Relations: The Cuban military has long maintained contact with the armed forces of developing world nations that are considered nonaligned or at least not ideologically hostile to the Castro regime. It was able to mitigate its post-Soviet isolation by developing closer ties with fellow military officers in Latin America and Europe, and its post–Cold War efforts to build contacts with foreign militaries were aided by Fidel Castro's 1992 declaration that Cuba would no longer support revolutionary movements abroad.

Russia still has a December 2000 agreement with Cuba to modernize Soviet-built Cuban military equipment, but there is little evidence that Cuba's inventory is being modernized. Perhaps the most important tie with a foreign military force to develop since the Soviet Union's demise has been the relationship with the Chinese Popular Liberation Army. In early 2001, China and Cuba concluded an agreement to increase military cooperation. However, the Chinese-Cuban military relationship, which appears to be more of a business arrangement, does not compare with Cuba's former military dependency on the Soviet Union.

External Threat: No neighboring Latin American or Caribbean countries pose a military threat to Cuba. The only country with a history of military intervention in Cuba since the expulsion of Spain in 1898 is the United States, which maintains the U.S. naval base at Guantánamo Bay, consisting of 1,600 army, 510 naval, 80 marine, and 65 air force personnel in 2004. The Castro government has always portrayed the United States in Cuban media as a potential military threat to Cuba, often using as an historical example the disastrous landing of an army of Cuban exiles organized by the U.S. Central Intelligence Agency on Playa Girón in the Bay of Pigs on the south-central Cuban coast on April 17, 1961. U.S. economic warfare against the island has always been a reality for the Castro government, which also portrays the U.S. threat as taking the form of support for internal subversion, human rights activism, and political interference. On August 1, 2006, claiming the country was "under threat" of U.S. aggression, Acting President Raúl Castro ordered a military mobilization of tens of thousands of reservists and militia members and the Special Troops as per plans that Fidel Castro "approved and signed on January 13, 2005."

Defense Budget: Cuba's defense budget shrank from 9.6 percent of gross domestic product (GDP) in 1985 to 2.8 percent of GDP in 1995. Over the past decade, it has remained under 4 percent of GDP. Cuba does not make public its defense spending, but expenditures on defense and internal security for 2005 were estimated at US$1.7 billion, compared with US$1.1 billion in 2003, US$900 million in 2002, US$789 million in 2001, and US$720 million in 1997. The 2003 estimate of US$1.1 billion was the equivalent of US$97 per head of population and US$23,157 per member of the armed forces. The army has become more self-reliant through greater involvement in the economy, particularly in agricultural food production, transport, and tourism (through the military-linked Gaviota Tourism Group, S.A.).

Major Military Units: The full establishment of a mobilized Cuban infantry division is 5,900 members; a mechanized division, 8,200; and an armored division, 6,200. A Cuban infantry regiment numbers 1,010 personnel, and each of its two battalions numbers 349 soldiers. Armored regiments consist of 720 personnel; each of their three tank battalions has about 110 soldiers and 21 tanks; artillery regiments have about 975 personnel. In early 2006, the army had four or five armored brigades, nine mechanized brigades, one airborne brigade, and one artillery group. In addition, the army included between 12 and 14 reserve infantry brigades. It was deployed regionally in the Western Army, Central Army, and Eastern Army. In addition, the Isla de la Juventud Military Region was garrisoned by forces equivalent to an infantry brigade. The Revolutionary Army Command included an airborne brigade and an artillery division. The Western Army included two mixed security regiments: one consisted of four divisions (brigade equivalents); the other, called the 2nd Pinar del Río Army Corps, consisted of three infantry divisions (brigades). The Central Army comprised three mixed security regiments, four infantry divisions (brigades), and the 4th Las Villas Army Corps, which consisted of three infantry brigades. The Eastern Army included 10 divisions (brigades), the Guantánamo Frontier Guard Brigade (comprising two infantry regiments), the 5th Holguín Army Corps (comprising one mechanized and four infantry divisions/brigades), and the 6th Camagüey Army Corps (consisting of one mechanized brigade and three infantry brigades).

Major military units of the rest of the armed forces also are divided into the western, central, and eastern regions. The three main territorial divisions of the air force and their responsible brigades are the Western Air Zone (the Bay Of Pigs Guard Brigade), the Central Air Zone (the Batalla de Santa Clara Guard Brigade), and the Eastern Air Zone (the Cuartel Moncada Guard Brigade). The nearly nonoperational navy, which is divided into the Western Naval District and the Eastern Naval District, has naval bases in Cabañas, Nicaro, Cienfuegos, Havana, Santiago de Cuba, and Banes.

Major Military Equipment: Although the army is well stocked with Russian equipment, much of it is obsolete or aging, and there is a critical shortage of spare parts. Most of Cuba's equipment came from the former Soviet Union and its East European allies, primarily Czechoslovakia and Poland. Under a 2000 accord, Russia is supposed to assist Cuba in modernizing its inventory. In the meantime, China has become Cuba's main supplier of arms.

Cuba reportedly has about 1,500 to 1,700 armored military vehicles in service. In 2005 the army inventory included an estimated 900 main battle tanks, including 400 T–62s (200 in service) and 1,100 T–54/55s (500 in service). Other armored vehicles included 50 PT–76 amphibious light tanks (30 in service), 100 BRDM–1/–2 reconnaissance vehicles (about 90 in service), 400 BMP–1 armored infantry fighting vehicles (about 150 in service), and 700 BTR–40/–50/–60/–152 armored personnel carriers (300 in service). The army's artillery included 37 self-propelled howitzers, 500 towed pieces, and about 175 BM–14 and BM–21 multiple rocket launchers. In addition, the army had 1,000 mortars.

The air force still has a sizable inventory, but it, too, suffers from obsolescence and critical shortages of spare parts. In 2006 the air force had 127 combat aircraft of Russian make, only about 25 of which were operational. The air force also had 87 Russian-made helicopters of various types. Air defense weapons included 300 low- to medium-altitude SAMs (surface-to-air missiles) of various types and antiaircraft guns of unknown quantities. As of 2006, the inventory included two new mobile versions of the Soviet-era S–75 (SA–2 Guideline) and S–125 (SA–3 Goa). Army aviation had about 65 Mi-type attack, utility, and antisubmarine warfare helicopters, about 63 of which were in service. Naval aviation included 18 Russian helicopters of unknown operational status. The navy also had a substantial but increasingly obsolescent inventory of equipment, which included about seven coastal patrol craft, four missile craft, six mine countermeasures craft, and one hydrographic survey vessel. Coastal defense equipment included the truck-mounted SS–N–2B Styx and various artillery pieces. Naval spare parts were in critical shortage.

Military Service: Since 1963 all male citizens between the ages of 16 and 45 have been liable for military service. The initial period of military training originally lasted three years, between the ages of 17 and 20. In 1991 active duty was reduced to a two-year tour. Reservists serve 45 days per year.

Paramilitary Forces: Active paramilitary forces totaled 26,500 in 2006. Paramilitary forces in general include a civil defense force of 50,000 and the Youth Labor Army (Ejército Juvenil de Trabajo—EJT). The EJT's membership ranges from 65,000 to 100,000, depending on the source but was approximately 70,000 in 2006. Primarily an organized labor force under the control of the Joint General Staff, the EJT has military training and equipment. By far the largest paramilitary force is the Territorial Troops Militia (Milicia de Tropas Territoriales—MTT), which is often described as having 1 million reservists. The MTT is organized into about 200 regiments comprising approximately 1,000 battalions. Primarily an infantry force, the MTT includes mounted units and some artillery and antiaircraft elements. The 6,500-member Border Guard Troops (Tropas de Guardafronteras—TGF) may also qualify as a paramilitary force.

Foreign Military Forces: Since 2000 the Chinese reportedly have operated two signals intelligence (SIGINT) facilities, located at Santiago de Cuba and Bejucal, for the purpose of monitoring military communications networks within the United States. All Russian combat troops have been withdrawn from Cuba, but some SIGINT troops and military advisers reportedly remain. The last major Russian presence on the island was the Lourdes SIGINT station; its announced closure in October 2001 deprived the Castro government of as much as US$200 million in annual rent.

Military Forces Abroad: The Cuban military does not participate in peace support operations and is not known to have any forces abroad, other than an unknown number of advisers in Venezuela. Since the mid-1990s, Cuba has sent Special Forces officers to Vietnam for training. Cuba reportedly considered a request from the government of the Solomon Islands in May 2000 for Cuban intervention in the interethnic civil war that was engulfing the islands. Cuba initially indicated a willingness to provide aid and support measures to help alleviate the fighting in return for diplomatic recognition and involvement in exploitation of the Pacific nation's mineral assets, but nothing came of the talks after regional diplomatic protests.

Security Forces: Civilian authorities control the security forces through the Ministry of Interior. However, most key positions in the ministry are held by officers of the Revolutionary Armed Forces. The security forces include the 20,000-member Department of State Security (Departamento de Seguridad del Estado—DSE), the Border Guard Troops (Tropas de Guardafronteras—TGF), and the 15,000-member National Revolutionary Police (Policía Nacional Revolucionaria—PRN). Reorganized in 1998, the PRN is known to be effective in its primary civil police role. Political control is exercised mainly through the DSE, which is supported by neighborhood block committees—Committees for the Defense of the Revolution (CDRs). The CDRs constitute a network of police informers and armed vigilantes that can be mobilized to intimidate opposition elements as well as to prevent crime. This network is headed by the national CDR, a component of the PRN. In addition, the Special Forces of the Ministry of Interior control Cuba's elite rapid-intervention force, consisting of two battalions of Special Troops (Tropas Especiales) that have a combined total strength of about 1,500. Highly trained and motivated, they appear to be extremely effective within the limitations of their small numbers. They are equipped with the best personal and close-support weapons available to the Cuban armed forces.

Internal Threats: The Castro regime's highly efficient secret services keep close control over public gatherings, are quick to quash any dissent, and closely monitor opposition groups. As a result, the Castro regime remains firmly in power and faces no serious internal threat to its power or stability or any signs of unrest resulting from the provisional transfer of power to Raúl Castro. That could change, however, if Raúl Castro, lacking his brother's charisma and stature, is unable to govern effectively in a post–Fidel Castro situation and is confronted by a power struggle. Currently, the only internal security threats are posed by street crime, organized crime, and illegal emigration. Although street crime has been rising, the crime rate is still lower than in other Latin American states, and the authorities have been making significant efforts to ensure that incidents do not adversely affect tourism. Nevertheless, some Cuban-American gangs reportedly are actively rebuilding their contacts in Cuba, and Cuba reportedly has a strong potential for a resurgence of organized crime, mainly related to drug trafficking, money laundering, and prostitution. Other transnational criminal networks including Russia-based groups have been establishing a presence on the island. The Italian police have reported that Sicilian organized crime is interested in developing operations in Cuba, seeking to use new construction projects related to the tourism industry to launder money. All forms of trafficking in persons are crimes in Cuba. Despite the absence of reports of human trafficking in Cuba in 2005, trafficking for underage prostitution and forced labor did occur.

Drug smuggling and illegal emigration are currently Cuba's principal maritime threats. Although Cuban policy is to prevent, intercept, and destroy drug contraband, the country's geographical position and limited coastal enforcement have not discouraged drug traffickers from transiting Cuban territorial water and airspace. Cuba aggressively pursues an internal narcotics enforcement, investigation, and prevention program and attempts to cooperate with the United States in narcotics enforcement areas. Nevertheless, Cuba is already an important trafficking transshipment point for drugs from Latin America and is unable to control its waters and airspace effectively. Most confiscations along the Cuban coastline come from the recovery of washed-up narcotics thrown overboard. Uncertainty regarding Fidel Castro's illness in early August 2006 prompted some U.S. concern over the threat of a new flood of illegal immigration to Florida in the wake of Castro's death, but no changes in U.S. immigration policy had resulted by mid-September.

Terrorism: According to the U.S. Department of State's annual terrorism report for 2005, Cuba continues "to embrace terrorism as an instrument of policy." Cuba has been on the department's list of states that sponsor terrorism since 1982, citing Fidel Castro's training and arming of communist rebels in Africa and Latin America. Since 1992, however, the regime appears to have ceased active military support of revolutionary groups in the absence of subsidies and other support from the former Soviet Union. Nevertheless, Cuba was the only nation that failed to condemn terrorism at the United Nations General Assembly session on November 16, 2001, and Cuba has continued to actively oppose the U.S.-led "war on terrorism" by taking a stance that "acts by legitimate national liberation movements cannot be defined as terrorism." Cuba has provided "limited support" to designated foreign terrorist organizations as well as haven for some terrorists such as members of the Basque terrorist group Fatherland and Freedom.

In past decades, Cuba was the target of anti-Castro terrorism by Florida-based Cuban exile groups. For example, Cuban exiles were linked to the firebombing of a Cubana airlines DC–8 jetliner that crashed off the coast of Barbados, killing all 73 persons aboard on October 6, 1976. Throughout the 1990s, Cuban-American exiles boasted of paramilitary raids into Cuba, including a series of hotel bombings in Havana in 1997. In 1999 two Salvadoran nationals were convicted of terrorism and sentenced to death for a string of hotel bombings carried out in 1997, in which one foreign tourist was killed. According to prosecutors, both the Salvadorans were acting on behalf of anti-Castro exiles trying to sabotage Cuba's tourism industry.

Human Rights: As a communist dictatorship, the Castro regime has a long record of disrespect for human rights, such as its draconian crackdown on dissidents in March–April 2003. The harsh prison sentences ranging from six to 28 years that were meted out to 75 human rights activists, independent journalists, and opposition figures set back the regime's efforts to win international and U.S. support for an end to economic and political sanctions. By the end of 2005, at least 333 Cuban political prisoners and detainees continued to be held in Cuba, according to the U.S. Department of State, but there were no known politically motivated killings or "disappearances." To legally repress dissent and restrict freedom of speech under the guise of protecting state security, the Castro regime relies on its Criminal Code, which criminalizes enemy propaganda, the spreading of "unauthorized news," and insults to patriotic symbols. Conditions in Cuba's overcrowded prisons continued to be harsh and life-threatening in 2005. Prison authorities frequently beat, neglected, isolated, and denied medical treatment to detainees and prisoners, particularly those convicted of political crimes or those who persisted in expressing their oppositional views. Authorities also often denied family visitation, adequate nutrition, exposure to natural light, pay for work, and the right to petition the prison director.